Unstuckable Part I

Helping You Renew Your Mind for Greatness & Success

MICHAEL D. BENEFIELD

ISBN:978-0-578-86899-8

Library of Congress Cataloging-in-Publication Data

Library of Congress Control Number:

Printed in the United States of America

First printing edition 2021.

This is a work of nonfiction. No names have been changed, no characters invented, no events were fabricated. Although the author and publisher have made every effort to ensure that the information in this book was correct at press time, the author and publisher do not assume and hereby disclaim any liability to any party for any loss, damage, or disruption caused by errors or omissions, whether such errors or omissions result from negligence, accident, or any other cause.

Contents

Preface

Welcome! First, I want to thank you for purchasing this book. This is the first step of many to help you on your self-awareness journey. There was something that compelled you to this book, and whatever that was, I'm very thankful for that reason. So, before we begin, I want to share a little bit of my story with you before we take a dive into this great content. This part of the book is very dear to my heart because this was the experience that helped me to push to get this book out to you. So, I've decided to share it with you in hopes that it will inspire, uplift, & motivate you towards greatness. I took myself back to this moment, and decided to add this story into it. I'm literally inviting you into my life. I know it will help you in more ways than I can imagine. So...Let's go!

Introduction

As I am writing this, I am in the neonatal unit with my wife, and a healthy baby girl who is trying to grow so we can take her home. She was born premature, and needed some assistance to help her grow properly. It was a scary day when she was born. My wife, and I were both nervous. Who knew a trip to the ER (Emergency Room) for my wife having high blood pressure would be the same day my baby girl was conceived? To hear the check-in nurse at one hospital say, "We are going to transport you to the hospital by ambulance," caused us to be confused. Now that I think about it, we were already at a hospital that could have treated her. I didn't know the exact reason, nor could have guessed it at that moment. I just went along with it while having so many feelings overwhelm me.

We finally arrived at the other hospital where her primary care doctor/OB-GYN works. I trailed the ambulance there anticipating what's going on. When I arrived, I was instructed to go to the labor, and delivery unit. As I got on the elevator I began to feel a series of emotions like, concern, worry, anger, anxiety, and so forth. When I arrived at the nurse's station, I asked "What room is Candy Benefield in?", They told me, and I think one nurse was showing me what room she was going to be in.

Before I could get down the hall, my wife was being wheeled in from the emergency entrance. So, I went to meet her, and the paramedics. Then, her doctor/OB-GYN followed behind a short distance, and put on a pair of plastic gloves and said "WE GOTTA DELIVER THIS BABY NOW!"

I immediately began to feel fear for my wife. This was her first time having a child, and for it to be told like that was frightening in itself to go back there with her but I was told by her OB-GYN, "You can't go back there. I don't want you to see her like that." He was implying that they had to put her under anesthesia, and do an emergency C-section. Boy, was i hot! I was angry because not only did I want to experience that with my wife, but I'm also a protector, and every man knows that term. So, I went back to the room the nurse originally brought me to, and threw the bags I had in my hands in anger. I came back out and thought of going in the room, then a nurse kindly told me "Please don't go in the room, I don't want anyone to get the police involved." I told her, "I DON'T CARE ABOUT NO POLICE!" My only concern was my wife's well-being and my unborn child. I was getting madder by the moment, until that same nurse told me, "It's going to be ok. Do you want to pray?" When she said that, it began to give me comfort in knowing who holds the future. We locked hands, and she said a sincere, and powerful prayer. After that moment, I was reminded of who I am, and what I was called to do as my wife's husband. I WAS CALLED TO PROTECT, AND PRAYER IS ALSO A WAY TO DO SO.

I then began to pace up and down the hall in front of the labor/delivery room she was in, just praying that everything goes smoothly. Then, moments later, I heard a baby cry. It was music to my ears. Shortly after, her doctor came out of the labor unit, and let me know everything went well. I told him "Thank you!" I was able to see my newborn daughter being surrounded by nurses, and getting weighed. I looked at her, then put my finger in her hand to see how strong her grip was. Needless to say, she had a grip like an Army Sergeant. So, I knew she was going to be ok in spite of being born two months prematurely. From there, they placed my wife in recovery. I was then able to go back there with her, kiss her on the forehead, and talk to her. But, there was one caveat - She had to stay in the hospital she gave birth in while our baby was transported to another hospital that has a NICU across town. During this time, which was 3-4 days, I had to travel back and forth to see her and my new born baby. I would spend all day with my wife, then before I headed home, I would go to the NICU, and FaceTime my wife so she could see our baby. It was a difficult time for us. Even when my wife was released, we still had to go home without our beautiful little baby girl (just a little FYI, it took us 7yrs to conceive). That's a whole different story we may have to write a book about together. Just imagine waiting that long to have an awesome

experience like that only for the story to say "*to be continued.*"
Well, that's how we felt.

I tried to be strong for my wife during this time while also dealing with my own emotional battles. It was a difficult time, but we stuck together. We felt emotions of stress, worry, fear, doubt, frustration, and more. Although we were having a difficult time trying to process that our princess was in the NICU, The Most High God was still showing us that we had no need to worry. I remember a time during that process we were low on money, and we found a gift card to a restaurant on the ground next to our car with enough money on it for both of us to eat. That was just one of many things I remember that happened. We were leaving the hospital from visiting our baby girl. I was on maternity leave from my job, and well, let's just say that didn't take care of everything. While walking outside to head home, we both felt hungry. We were exhausted, and so were our finances, but there it was, a restaurant gift card on the ground by the driver's side door! I normally see gift cards lying around everywhere, but this time I picked this one up. I immediately called the number to see if anything was on it, and to our surprise there was more than enough money on it for the both of us to eat. Some may call it luck, but we like to call it a **blessing**.

That incident let me and my wife know that we have come too far to give up. Me and my wife continued to travel back and forth to the NICU for the next 3 months or so, until our baby got her weight up. As the days went by, we experienced more emotional moments. She cried all the time because we couldn't take her home, and I was crying because the experience was beautiful in more ways than I can express. I literally cried all the time, but there was another feeling that started to cultivate during this time. I began to look at my baby girl, and wanted to give her the world. I felt like I wanted to give her everything she wanted and more. I realized that she didn't ask to be born to us, so I needed to make sure I wouldn't cheat her in any way by not reaching to become a better version of me. I had a YouTube channel that I had started, and a couple other things I was working on - including this book. I didn't understand much about any of it, but I was willing to avoid procrastinating and learn because I now have someone else who is depending on me (even more than my wife) to make moves. My wife is also a big part of me pushing me to be the best I can be as well. I pursued everything I started before she was born times 2, including writing this book that I am sure will help you in ways you couldn't imagine.

Now, the real work begins. Let's get started!

Affirmation & Prayer

AFFIRMATION (say this everyday):

I was created to be more than average. Although I have failed, I am not a failure. Everything in my life up to this point has taught me something. They were not mistakes, but life lessons that will help catapult me into my destiny. The vision that God has blessed me with, and given me shall come to pass. I will not look at what I don't have, but I will use the resources I have, such as the Internet, books, YouTube, and Google to help teach me. These things will help me solve any issues I have until I find a mentor. I may feel lost in many ways, but I am not lost. I am on my way to greatness and NO ONE NOR NOTHING CAN STOP IT.

Prayer & Decree (say this aloud):

God I come to you now, asking that you will give me the strength and courage to move forward in life. I don't know all that it takes, but I know you will and can give me the wisdom I need to make the right decisions. Forgive me for doubting you in any way. I ask that you remove all doubt, fear, double-mindedness, stress, insecurity, and anxiety from my life. I ask that you show me how to use all the necessary learning tools I have access to. I pray that you give me the power to fight past my distractions, and feelings of being too old, or not good enough.

I decree and declare I have power, might and strength. That I am more than a conqueror through Christ Jesus that strengthens me. I refuse to live an ordinary life because You have created me to be more. I decree that I am a leader and not a follower, I am a lender and not a borrower. I pray that as you mature me in my moving forward that I won't get weary, and that you will be my strength. I am blessed because of my obedience in moving forward, my family is blessed, and everyone that I come in contact with is blessed. I decree that every generational curse is broken from over my life and my family members' lives. My past is behind me and my future is in your hands. In Jesus name, I pray, Amen!

I want you to take a minute and reflect on that affirmation and prayer. Absorb it, breathe it, become one with it. That was an affirmation and prayer from my heart to you to give you strength, hope, and resilience to move forward in your endeavors. I also have included reflective questions after each chapter for you to answer. This book is yours to write in. The answers you place here are for your own eyes to see, unless you feel comfortable enough to share with someone who needs help in an area you are currently in or that you have overcome. It gives you something to scale - aka something to look back on. I believe it can be a healing, yet life changing experience for you. This is a part of self-awareness. As you begin to grow on your journey, you will begin to see yourself in a way you have never done before. It will almost be as if you are reading about another person, but it's actually you. This exercise will, and can help you if you are honest with the process. Understand, and know you are free from judgement, shame, guilt and any other feeling that tries to tell you that you can't move forward in life. Be truthful in the journey and the results will be like something you have never experienced before.

Oftentimes in life, the average person doesn't know the gifts that they possess. The average person spends their life working for someone else, or going to school to end up working for someone else. In today's society, the average person's success is measured by 1 of 3 things: How much money they make a year, their career, or how many . social media followers they have. "Although all these may be true, they may not all apply to you." Mostly everyone reading this can agree that they have had one of these encounters, or know someone who has or currently is dealing with this "status quo." It makes you question life and wonder, "Is there more to my life?", Others may say, "I know that there is more to my life, but where do I start?" If this is you or has been you at some point in your life, there is hope and a bright future for you. You were not created to fit in or blend in. You were created to be more than average.

I

Finding Out Who You Are

The average human being already knows they want to become, even at a young age. Have you ever asked a kid, "What do you want to be when you grow up?" Well, if you have, you know that most of them have an idea of what they want to be, (or, at least what they want to do) when they grow up. The sad truth with this is that a large percentage of these kids will not do the thing they want to do. Some of them won't because they will have unforeseen circumstances that may stop them from graduating high school, or even finishing middle school, others may have graduated high school, and just decide that's all they want out of the school system, and some may have finished college only to find out they hate what they earned a degree in. One of these examples may have been you, and may not have been you. Even if they were, you are able to still find the God-given purpose and passion that is within you.

At some point in a person's life, they ask themselves, "Is there more to my life?" I can say I honestly asked myself this, and often felt like a failure when the answer didn't present itself fast enough. Have you ever felt lost? Clueless?

Desperate for change? Well, you and me both. The good thing is you don't have to stay there and feel this way for too long. Think back to when you were a kid, or at least to when you had an idea of what you wanted to do with your life. Now look at where you are currently. Is this where you want to be? Or, could you see yourself doing something completely different?

If you answered yes, let's get to it. I once heard a mentor ask me this question, "What is one thing you can do every day of your life and not get paid?" When this question was presented to me, it made me think. I mean, it made me really think! To be honest with you, the first thing I did was think about what I *wanted* to do and not what I was **created** to do. You might be asking, "What do you mean?" Well, remember earlier how the three things were mentioned, I thought about question number two, which was my career. I had an idea of what I wanted to do that paid decent money, and what I thought I may be good at, but the thought of how much money I wanted to make was overshadowing my "purpose."

This was a messed up way of thinking, because money should never be the primary motivational reason for you doing what you love to do. I mean, you should want to make money, and not work for free, but you don't want the thought of how much you make to overshadow the love, passion, and creativity God has placed within you. I'll explain this later on in the book. In today's society, the average person is working a job that they don't like, and the only reason they are still there is because of the money they make. This may not be you. You may feel like you are fine at the company you work for, but ask yourself this honest question, "Is this all that I am created to do?" If you said no, then it's time to get to work.

Reflective moments

1. After reading this chapter, what did it make you think about concerning yourself, or in general?

2. How did this chapter make you feel?

3. What were some of the key points for you?

4. What do you honestly feel you've been created to do?

5. Are you doing or pursuing anything around this? There is no correct or incorrect answer.

(Hint: others can eventually benefit from it just as well as you.)

Unstuckable Part I

Michael D. Benefield

II

Gradual Steps

Now, we are at the part of the book that I'd like to call "crawling." I know what you may be saying. "Why is he calling it crawling when the chapter is called GRADUAL STEPS!" Well, there is a reason for that. Before a baby can walk, they have to crawl. This is considered gradual because it's a part of the process to get them to walk. Many people in today's society thrive off of popularity and what's trending. Although it's good to not live under a rock, it is also not good to allow your eyes to be bigger than what's in your bank account. When I first decided to venture out and create a brand, I had to be real with myself and where I was in life. I say that to say this: Go after what's in your heart and not after what you see! It can be very easy to read articles about how several successful people are living, but the part most don't absorb is all the hard times they hit, how they filed bankruptcy, how they were homeless, and how friends and family turned their back on them.

I've always been one to check the backstory of someone I admire. This helps me not to get anxious while I am venturing out on something new. If you can see where someone has come from to get to where they are, it will help you build a level of gratitude while you are taking your "gradual steps." I didn't realize this before stepping out and it caused me a great deal of stress. I felt like I had something to prove, so I went after the words of those in my past that told me "You will never be anything." I was functioning out of a place that caused me to want to go from "nothing to something" overnight, and that can be considered a distraction in many ways.

I once heard a great man say "It's a marathon, and not a sprint," and that's the way you have to look at everything you will strive after in life. The mindset of a champion realizes that all good things take time. Anything worth having is worth fighting for. I want you to look back over your life and thank God for those things you considered failures. You see half of the things we know now, and have learned have come from most of the mistakes we have made. That's what all the greats have done. I've read countless stories of different athletes and people who learn from their downfalls. During the process of getting from where you are to the desired place you want to get to it takes time.

You will feel like quitting, and throwing in the towel. I've been there, and even face those feelings at times now when venturing out on something new, but I don't quit. If you can see it then it's yours. I know I'm not the only one who can see myself doing something before I'm actually doing it. It's called VISION, and many people don't act upon their God given vision because of fear, and some of the things you will read in this book. Even reading this book is a gradual step of many that you are taking to get to operating in those visions you have.

Look at it this way: Every step you take is a lesson you learn that nobody can steal from you. Once you have acquired the knowledge, all you have to do is apply it. It's almost like a recipe, each and every ingredient plays a major part in making the dish complete. If you remove something, it may not taste the same. If you add something, it may not taste the same -which either is fine, but you may not get the desired results you want. In other words, there are no shortcuts when trying to get the desired results you want.

When pursuing any endeavor, you must realize that it won't happen overnight. But, with the right mindset and ambition, success is possible. Everybody you see doing something amazing had to start where you are right now. Don't think just because they may have a huge following and a lot of notoriety that it happened in an instant, because it didn't (like I stated earlier). Look at it this way the small steps (investments) you are making now will help you to reap big returns later. You just have to stay focused, be present, and not get caught up with things that can be potential distractions.

REFLECTIVE MOMENTS

1. After reading this chapter what did it make you think about concerning yourself, or in general?

2. How did this chapter make you feel?

3. What were some of the key points for you?

4. What are some gradual steps you are taking right now, or that you plan to take in the near future? Also how will they benefit you?

Unstuckable Part I

Michael D. Benefield

III

Blocking Out Distractions

N ow this chapter will go a little different. I want you to close your eyes and think hard. Think hard about all possible distractions. This can be people, Facebook, Instagram, Twitter, or anything that is wasting your time in a non-beneficial way, or in other words in a way that will cause you to be distracted. Let's be honest with ourselves, Facebook is the next news station always reporting live, and Instagram is always painting perfect pictures of people's lives, but hiding in pain, shame, and hurt - amongst many other illusions. This alone can make you feel as if you are less than a person, or like your life is all jacked up. I can honestly say for years I have sat back and watched other people's lives and thought to myself "My life sucks."

I said it to myself so much, that I started to actually believe it. I would always be so concerned with other's success stories, that I couldn't see I was worthy enough to have my own. You may not have a Facebook, Instagram or Twitter account, but maybe you have looked at someone else's life and felt this way. Well guess what? Me too. But, I got enough strength and courage to fight off negative thoughts and feelings, and so can you. A scripture that I have always kept in my heart is (Romans 12:2 - And be not conformed to this world: but be ye transformed by the renewing of your mind, that ye may prove what [is] that good, and acceptable, and perfect, will of God). What does this mean to you? What can you gain from this?

The good thing is that when you read that scripture, it gives some type of thought. Well, that's the same way distractions work. If a picture can be implanted in your mind - good or bad, it can have an effect on you. There is one thing that everyone must understand, and it is "Your perception is "your world!" How you perceive things can either make you or break you. Don't take everything on like it is your life or your problem.

This can be how you view other's lives, or the problems other people can bring you. Don't allow family members, friends, or social media to place you in a box of "distractions." Your time is valuable, and so is your life. So the next time you start to feel less than what God created you to be, "step back." Ask yourself, *"Is this helping me move toward my goals, visions, and dreams?"* If not, then block it out. There will be times that people who are negative will come your way.

They will make mockery out of you trying to better yourself. They can see that you are trying to better yourself, but choose to distract you. You have finally decided that you are going to get back in school, and here they come, inviting you to a party the first week you are in school. It never fails that as soon as you start to better yourself, people and their distractions come out of nowhere. It's time for you to identify what are your distractions, and get to working in your God given potential.

Reflective moments

1. After reading this chapter, what did it make you think about concerning yourself, or in general?

2. How did this chapter make you feel?

3. What were some of the key points for you? How can you apply them in your life?

4. What are some things you feel are distracting you?

5. What are some things you can do to not allow those things to not affect you as easily moving forward?

Michael D. Benefield

Unstuckable Part I

IV

Get Started (It's Never Too Late)

I'm ready to start", is what you say, whether it be learning an instrument, writing a book, going back to school, starting a business, or even bettering yourself as a person. Then all of a sudden, you find yourself feeling like it's a waste of time. Well, at least give yourself a pat on the back. You are a lot further than some who thinks about it, but never acts on it. Maybe you are the one who has thought about it, but just haven't acted upon it. If so, either way you are on your way to doing something most don't have the courage to do.

That one thing is "GETTING STARTED!" You may be saying, "Well, I haven't actually done anything yet." But one thing you have to know is, before anything becomes reality, you have to think it first. The majority of the world is founded on someone who had an idea. They not only had an idea, but they acted upon it. Don't be one of the ones who has a world changing idea but does nothing with it.

Many thoughts can come up during your process of wanting to bring an idea to life. You may begin and feel great, and then all of a sudden, here comes the negative thoughts. The feelings of worthlessness, anxiousness, giving up, and even IM TOO OLD, and I DON'T HAVE ENOUGH MONEY. It's all normal and part of the process. I remember when I first started to learn guitar. I first started almost a year after I got married.

At that time I gave up because of the thoughts I had consisted of those negative thoughts and more. I felt that I was too old (take note I was only in my 20's). I was distracted, unfocused, and a huge overthinker, but God's grace kicked in for me 7 years later. It's funny how we end right back where we left off. Have you ever been working towards something, put it off a few years, then end up facing it again later in life? Well, me too, and that is what happened with me. I left guitar, and 7 years passed by and I was back on it.

During this time, I was finding out more about myself and what God was putting back into my heart to do. I was at work one day and heard God tell me as clear as day, "Get back on your guitar." I immediately called my wife while I was still at work and explained this to her. She understood me because I've always been obedient in moving when God places something on my heart. At that time, all I had was a credit card to purchase the guitar. I purchased a low-end practice guitar, because that's all I needed. My wife didn't think it was a good idea to use my credit card at the time, but I knew what God put in my heart. Therefore, I needed to act fast. I purchased the guitar and haven't looked back since.

I went on to learn all I could learn between YouTube and getting actual lessons. I was also able to be a part of a worship leader guitar program, and was selected to go to a Maverick City music songwriting camp because I had taken my guitar seriously, and began to follow what God had placed in my heart. I met several musician friends along the way, and other awesome things. I don't know where I would be right now if I didn't go back and learn the guitar. I've always sang since I was a child, but to be able to learn an instrument years later only made it better. There was a musician that I forgot to mention, whom I met through a mutual friend of someone else I knew.

The funny thing is I met him the first time I gave up on the guitar, but I didn't reach out to him until after the 7-year break. Weird, I know. But goes to show you, how you will end right back where you left off. I could have easily told myself the next time around, that I don't have the money, I can't figure things out, or even I'm too old. I thought all those things and although I felt they were true, they weren't!! Getting started can seem like a daunting task, but to the majority of us, it's second nature. Just imagine if I didn't move when I knew I should have. I would have never made the connections, or had those doors of opportunity open for me. The thoughts came, and feelings, but I was determined to get started. Don't allow a feeling to determine how far you are willing to go in life. The majority of the time, your feelings come from a place of insecurity in yourself. Go into it already seeing yourself winning the victory. All good things take time, but with persistence, consistency, and a made-up mind, nothing is impossible. If I never would have decided to act upon what God placed in my heart, I would have not done some of those awesome things, or even written this book. That one thing led to so many other things because it was a piece of the puzzle. The very thing you could be putting off could potentially lead to so many great things you never thought were possible.

Reflective moments

1. After reading this chapter, what did it make you think about concerning yourself, or in general?

2. How did this chapter make you feel?

3. What were some of the key points for you? How can you apply them in your life?

4. What are some things you have been putting off that you know you need to pursue?

Michael D. Benefield

Unstuckable Part I

V

Invest In Yourself (The 3 R's)

B y now you should have noticed something. I'm sure you have, and I'm sure you learned several things as well. But, there is one thing I want you to get out of this specifically, and that is "invest in yourself." You owe it to yourself to do the 3 R's. Which is 1. Read, 2. Research, and 3. Reach Out. I recommend doing these things, because they will give you clarity. Oftentimes, when we are in the process of building, we don't see all the possibilities we could have. Let's be honest, when we are starting out on a venture, we think it's supposed to happen overnight. (Or at least our actions show it) During the process, we often forget that it takes time. Remember, a new born baby can't walk before learning to crawl.

The same principle applies to anyone who wants to build or is already building something. No matter if you are going back to school, starting a business, or building an influential brand - IT TAKES TIME!! I often forgot this, and when I did, I stressed myself out. I had to understand that I needed to take it one day at a time. This helped me to have clarity and balance when I began to build in different areas of my life. I started to invest in myself by learning what I needed to learn, and reaching out to those who I knew could help me along the way. Never try to figure things out on your own. Google, YouTube, and Yahoo will be and can be your best friends.

The stress of feeling like you need to have all the money in the world will come. Even then, you have to step back and look at all you have, and what you have to work with. Small investments can go a long way. Even 5 dollars can eventually turn into 1000 dollars if you save it long enough. It is important that you learn how to use small investments to make big results. You aren't just living to pay bills, be another college graduate, or another 9-5 employee. If you work a 9-5 job, you owe it to yourself to invest something out of each paycheck you get. If you have any type of money coming in, don't be afraid to invest some of it back into your God given dream.

Ask those who you may see doing what you're desiring to do, the necessary questions. Get advice, tips, and strategies to help you. Just make sure if you are reaching out to an individual or individuals, they have the fruit in their lives in some type of way. How many times have you taken advice from an individual or individuals who have no clue what they are talking about? They are just talking because it sounds good. Their intentions may be right, but you can't afford to thrive off of their good intentions. YOU NEED FRUIT (AKA PROOF). I've always admired individuals who are in a space that I am desiring to be. To be honest with you, I have reached out to a few of them, and they have responded. I would advise you to do the same. The next time you see someone online, or a person that you admire, reach out to them. If they don't respond back, don't be offended. Some of them have very busy lifestyles, and you are one of many wanting guidance in an area. Some may communicate with you, some may have a team to do so, and some may have courses you can take. There are several ways of getting the knowledge you need. You may not have all the money you need, but you can use what you have to get going. Also, if you need mentorship from me, I would love to help you on your journey. Just visit www.mymentor.life/michaelbenefield and book a session. Also you can DM me on Instagram @ https://www.instagram.com/michaeldbenefield. Now I can't coach in the DM so it's best to book, but I can briefly answer a concern. Make the investment in yourself. You are worth it! At the end of the day, you can't depend on friends, family, or anyone else because they may fail you. If God gave you the vision, 9 times out of 10, He has given you the tools to carry it out. Overthinking happens, and most of the time it's us, getting in our own way. Don't do that! Learn and grow, and move your negative thoughts out of the way. Have patience, invest, and trust the process. If I never learned anything out of investing in myself, I learned this. The Bible says in James 1:17, "Every good and perfect thing comes from the above." Once I realized that about my God given vision, building it felt a little less stressful. Plant your seeds of time, money, and labor, and you will witness the harvest it will yield.

Reflective moments

1. After reading this chapter, what did it make you think about concerning yourself, or in general?

2. How did this chapter make you feel?

3. What were some of the key points for you? How can you apply them in your life?

4. How have you invested in yourself thus far?

5. What ways are you looking to invest in yourself to get the results you desire?

Unstuckable Part I

VI

What Is Your Why? Pursue Intentional Greatness

T his chapter is the icing on any cake. I honestly believe it also puts all the other chapters in perspective. I want you to ask yourself this question: "What changes do I want to see in my life, my children's lives (if you have any), my family member's life, or changes you want to see in the world?" I asked you that question because that is something many people don't think about, and if they do, it's surface level. Some may say, "I want to make more money, others may say "I just want to be able to help others out"! While these are great responses from individuals, they often speak from a place of uncertainty and impulse. Their heart is there, but the emotion and desire isn't strong enough to push them into action to make these things happen. Think back to when you were younger. You were often posed this question, "What do you want to be when you grow up?" Some of the answers would be a doctor, a teacher, a professional athlete, a lawyer, and so forth. Although these are great answers, and purpose can be found in those things, that's not usually the first reason children, or even adults want to pursue one of those careers. Remember what I talked about in the very first chapter of the book? As you grow older, things begin to change, such as your outlook on life. What you thought you wanted to do with your life doesn't seem so interesting anymore, as it probably did when you were younger, or even now. Some have actually found one of those professions to be very purposeful for them, and others that may have discovered they don't like doing it anymore. I mean the money is good, they are able to get what they want when they want, but it's not what they feel they have been created to do. I have heard numerous stories about individuals who worked in corporate America, and left to walk into a 6-7 figure purposeful entrepreneurial life. That's not to say that being in one of those professions I mentioned earlier can't bring that same life, but make sure you are being true to yourself, and not selling yourself short. Something must trigger your "WHY" to help you not just live, but live intentional. Let's say for instance you begin to notice that everyone in your family always gets jobs, retires from them, and collects retirement. You, on the other hand, began to look at that and say, "Why do they decide to not pursue anything outside of a 9-5 when they are gifted at let's say writing, cleaning, or maybe even decorating?" That question alone will be enough to fire you up where you will begin to question your own life. And it should. Have you ever been here before? If not, I'm glad I put it in perspective for you. I know we have already discussed so many topics in this book so far that I know has opened your mind up to a new level of thinking. At the very beginning of the book, as you may remember, I talked about me and my wife's experience at the NICU. That experience alone was enough to have me question where I was headed with my life. I didn't want to cheat my daughter, let alone my kids and wife because I wasn't willing to pursue greatness. Sometimes, honestly, well a lot of times, you have to be the change you want to see. You may look and wonder why all the people around you are doing the same thing - Grabbing coffee, rushing in traffic to get to work, clocking out, and going home all just to do it again tomorrow. I'm not knocking anyone who chooses to do that, but there comes a time in every person's life where they should ask themselves, "Is there more to my life than this?" I know for me that was something I asked myself quite often, and I'm glad I did. On your own self-discovery journey, you will see that you have been cheating yourself this whole time in many ways unknowingly. Some of you reading this right now are great at so many things, but choose to sit on it because you don't think you can't go far or excel with it. I felt the exact way before I got to the place I am now. Every time I looked around, I would see individuals doing some of the same things I knew I was good at. I would see them and say, "What makes me any different?" I knew I had what it took to be one of the ones doing what I saw, so I went for it in my own way. It can be so easy to see others doing something you are good at, and compare yourself to them. My advice to you is to not copy them, or envy them, but admire them while trying to find your own feel for your gifting. This will help you to stay motivated while learning how to apply/use your gift to bring forth a change you desire to see. You must understand that although there are people doing the same exact thing you desire to do/or are doing, they aren't you. Your fingerprint is unique, and no one else has it but you. Are you content with where you are in life? Do you know what your why is? Do you know there is another level of greatness in your life that you haven't seen? Are you ready to live intentionally? I ask those questions because I want you to answer the call of greatness in your life. Don't just go through the motions of routine and allow your life to just pass you by. You are not in a race with anyone. Every day is a new day to ask yourself those questions and begin to pursue what's in your heart. You have someone depending on you, whether you believe it or not. Understand, with you making the first step outside of your comfort zone you are giving hope to someone else that didn't think it was possible. There are kids that need you to be the change they need whether or not they are yours. That man or woman needs you to show them what it means to not live in a cycle, or rat race. Those family members you may see living in a cycle need you to show them that there is more. People respond to your actions better than your words. This is not to say you have something to prove to them. They just need someone close to them to begin to break out of complacency. It may just rub off on them! Whether or not it does is up to them though. You have to do it for you, and those who you know may be depending on you. You have already seen yourself doing major things, I'm sure. That's called vision, and the Most High God didn't give it to you for nothing. It's meant for you to pursue. You may be the first person in your family to start a 6-7 figure business. You may be the first to write a book in your family. Whatever it is, you have been given the vision to do it because it requires your fingerprint. Nobody has access to it but you! While you are pursuing greatness, remember the points given in this book. They will help you to not lose sight of why you are starting in the first place. Don't believe the lies that try to come in your head like, "I'm not good enough," "I'm too old," or "Nobody will support me." Trust me, I've had all those thoughts with everything that I've ventured out on, but those are considered distractions as well. Thoughts like that always come when you are venturing out into a place of the unknown. There are people who need what you have, and how you deliver it. So, pursue greatness and do it intentionally. Michael D. Benefield

Reflective moments

1. After reading this chapter what did it make you think about concerning yourself or in general?

2. How did this chapter make you feel?

3. What were some of the key points for you? How can you apply them in your life?

4. What is your why?

Michael D. Benefield

Unstuckable Part I

VII

Motivation Mindset Conclusion

U se what you have, don't overthink. You may only have a few dollars to your name, or you might have money, just no vision. Either way, you can make something happen. Don't let another year, month, week, day, hour, minute or second go by. It's time for you to go and get what's yours. Make up in your mind I will not settle for less, I will not sit by and allow myself to live in complacency. Once you get sick and tired of being sick and tired, you will make a change. I challenge you to be better. You are not a product of mistakes, misfortune, or defeat. Every day is another day to be great. You may not be where you want to be in life, but you are not where you used to be. Tell yourself every day, "I will be all I can be, and more." Now, it's your turn to be "MORE THAN AVERAGE." GO GET WHAT'S YOURS!!

Michael D. Benefield

Thank You

I thank you for making it to the end of the book. This book was birthed out of my unwillingness to be fearful.

There are people depending on me such as my wife, children, and others I may not know. When God gave me this book, I wrote it with you in mind. You decided to purchase this book for a reason. This shows me that you take your life more seriously and you want all that God has for you and more.

Send me a message on Instagram: www.instagram.com/michaeldbenefield Or email me at support@createdtobemore.com, and let me know your thoughts and how this has helped you in any way. I would love to hear from you.